REFERENCES

Simpson, J. A., Rholes, W. S., & Phillips, D. (1996). Conflict in close relationships: An attachment perspective. *Journal of Personality and Social Psychology, 71*, 899–914.

Smedema, S. M., Chan, J. Y., & Phillips, B. N. (2014). Core self-evaluations and Snyder's hope theory in persons with spinal cord injuries. *Rehabilitation Psychology, 59*, 399–406.

Smirnova, M., & Parks, A. C. (2017). Positive psychology interventions: Clinical applications. In D. S. Dunn (Ed.), *Positive psychology: Established and emerging issues* (pp. 276–297). Routledge.

Smith, C. A., Organ, D. W., & Near, J. P. (1983). Organizational citizenship behavior: Its nature and antecedents. *Journal of Applied Psychology, 68*, 653–663.

Smith, M. L., Bergeron, C. D., Cowart, C., Ahn, S. N., Towne, S. D., Jr., Ory, M. G., ... Chaney, J. D. (2017). Factors associated with ageist attitudes among college students. *Geriatrics & Gerontology International, 17*(10), 1698–1706.

Smith, P. B. (2019). Changes in reported nation-level pro-social behavior frequencies over 6 years: A test of alternative predictors. *Social Indicators Research, 144*, 1195–1208.

Smith, T. W., Pope, M. K., Rhodewalt, F., & Poulton, J. L. (1989). Optimism, neuroticism, coping, and symptom reports: An alternative interpretation of the Life Orientation Test. *Journal of Personality and Social Psychology, 56*, 640–648.

Snyder, C. R. (1994). *The psychology of hope: You can get there from here.* Free Press.

Snyder, C. R. (1997). Control and the application of Occam's Razor to terror management theory. *Psychological Inquiry, 8*, 48–49.

Snyder, C. R. (2002). Hope theory: Rainbows in the mind. *Psychological Inquiry, 13*, 249–275.

Snyder, C., Harris, C., Anderson, J. R., Holleran, S. A., Irving, L. M., Sigmon, S. T., ... Harney, P. (1991). The will and the ways: Development and validation of an individual-differences measure of hope. *Journal of Personality and Social Psychology, 60*(4), 570.

Snyder, C. R., Berg, C., Woodward, J. T., Gum, A., Rand, K. L., Wrobleski, K. K., ... Hackman, A. (2005). Hope against the cold: Individual differences in trait hope and acute pain tolerance on the cold p[...]
Personality, 73, 287–312.

Snyder, C. R., & Feldman, D. B. (2000). Hope for the many: An empowering social agenda. In C. R. Snyder (Ed.), *Handbook of hope: Theory, measures, and applications* (pp. 389–412). Academic Press.

Snyder, C. R., Feldman, D. B., Taylor, J. D., Schroeder, L. L., & Adams, V. H., III. (2000). The roles of hopeful thinking in preventing problems and enhancing strengths. *Applied and Preventive Psychology, 9*(4), 249–269.

Snyder, C. R., Michael, S. T., & Cheavens, J. S. (1999). Hope as a psychotherapeutic foundation of nonspecific factors, placebos, and expectancies. In M. A. Huble, B. Duncan, & S. Miller (Eds.), *Heart and soul of change: What works in therapy* (pp. 205–230). American Psychological Association.

Snyder, C. R., Rand, K., King, E., Feldman, D. B., & Woodward, J. T. (2002). "False" hope. *Journal of Clinical Psychology, 58*, 1003–1022.

Sorokowski, P., Sorokowska, A., Karwowski, M., Groyecka, A., Aavik, T., Akello, G., ... Atama, C. S. (2020). Universality of the triangular theory of love: Adaptation and psychometric properties of the triangular love scale in 25 countries. *The Journal of Sex Research.* Advance online publication. https://doi.org/10.1080/00224499.2020.1787318

Sparks, E. A., & Baumeister, R. F. (2008). If bad is stronger than good, why focus on human strength. *Positive Psychology: Exploring the Best in People, 1*, 55–79.

Sprecher, S., & Hatfield, E. (2017). The importance of love as a basis of marriage: Revisiting Kephart (1967). *Journal of Family Issues, 38*, 312–335.

Stack, S., & Eshleman, J. R. (1998). Marital status and happiness: A 17 nation study. *Journal of Marriage and the Family, 60*, 527–536.

Stangier, U., Hilling, C., Heidenreich, T., Risch, A. K., Barocka, A., Schlösser, R., ... Weck, F. (2013). Maintenance cognitive-behavioral therapy and manualized psychoeducation in the treatment of recurrent depression: A multicenter prospective randomized controlled trial. *American Journal of Psychiatry, 170*, 624–632.

Stangor, C., & McMillan, D. (1992). Memory for expectancy-congruent and expectancy-incongruent information: A review of the social and social developmental literatures. *Psychological Bulletin, 111,* 42–61.

Statista. (2020). *College enrollment in the United States from 1965 to 2018 and projections up to 2029 for public and private colleges.* www.statista.com/statistics/183995/us-college-enrollment-and-projections-in-public-and-private-institutions/

Steenbergen-Hu, S., Makel, M. C., & Olszewski-Kubillus, P. (2016). What one hundred years of research says about the effects of ability grouping and acceleration on K-12 students' academic achievement: Findings of two second-order meta-analyses. *Review of Educational Research, 86,* 849–899.

Steger, M. (2012). Experiencing meaning in life: Optimal functioning at the nexus of well-being, psychopathology, and spirituality. In P. T. Wong (Ed.), *The human quest for meaning* (2nd ed., pp. 165–184). Routledge.

Steger, M. F., & Dik, B. J. (2009). If one is looking for meaning in life, does it help to find meaning in work? *Applied Psychology: Health and Well-Being, 1,* 303–320.

Steger, M. F., Frazier, P., Oishi, S., & Kaler, M. (2006). The Meaning in Life Questionnaire: Assessing the presence of and search for meaning in life. *Journal of Counseling Psychology, 53,* 80–93.

Steger, M. F., Hicks, B. M., Kashdan, T. B., Kruegger, R. F., & Bouchard, T. J., Jr. (2007). Genetic and environmental influences on the positive traits of the values in action classification and biometric covariance with normal personality. *Journal of Research in Personality, 41,* 524–539.

Steger, M. F., Oishi, S., & Kashdan, T. B. (2009). Meaning in life across the life span: Levels and correlates of meaning in life from emerging adulthood to older adulthood. *Journal of Positive Psychology, 4*(1), 43–52.

Steger, M. F., Oishi, S., & Kesebir, S. (2011). Is a life without meaning satisfying? The moderating role of the search for meaning in satisfaction with life judgments. *The Journal of Positive Psychology, 6,* 173–180.

Stellar, J. E., John-Henderson, N., Anderson, C. L., Gordon, A. M., McNeil, G. D., & Keltner, D. (2015). Positive affect and markers of inflammation: Discrete positive emotions predict lower levels of inflammatory cytokines. *Emotion, 15,* 129–133.

Stephens, G. J., Silbert, L. J., & Hasson, U. (2010). Speaker–listener neural coupling underlies successful communication. *Proceedings of the National Academy of Sciences, 107*(32), 14425–14430.

Steptoe, A., Wardle, J., Marmot, M., & McEwan, B. S. (2005). Positive affect and health-related neuroendocrine, cardiovascular, and inflammatory processes. *Proceedings of the National Academy of Sciences, 102,* 6508–6512.

Sternberg, R. J. (1996). The costs of expertise. In K. A. Ericsson (Ed.), *The road to excellence: The acquisition of expert performance in the arts and sciences, sports, and games* (pp. 347–354). Erlbaum.

Stillman, T. F., & Baumeister, R. F. (2009). Uncertainty, belongingness, and four needs for meaning. *Psychological Inquiry, 20,* 249–251.

Stocks, E. L., Lishner, D. A., & Decker, S. K. (2009). Altruism or psychological escape: Why does empathy promote prosocial behavior? *European Journal of Social Psychology, 39,* 649–665.

Stone, A. A., Schneider, S., & Broderick, J. E. (2017). Psychological stress declines rapidly from age 50 in the United States: Yet another well-being paradox. *Journal of Psychosomatic Research, 103,* 22–28.

Strauss, C., Cavanagh, K., Oliver, A., & Pettman, D. (2014). Mindfulness-based interventions for people diagnosed with a current episode of an anxiety or depressive disorder: A meta-analysis of randomized controlled trials. *PLoS ONE, 9,* e96110.

Strauss, K., & Parker, S. K. (2014). Effective and sustained proactivity in the workplace: A self-determination theory perspective. In M. Gagne (Ed.), *Oxford library of psychology: The Oxford handbook of work engagement, motivation, and self-determination theory* (pp. 50–71). Oxford University Press.

Strawbridge, W. J., Wallhagen, M. I., & Cohen, R. D. (2002). Successful aging and well-being: Self-rated compared with Rowe and Kahn. *The Gerontologist, 42*, 727–733.

Stubbe, J. H., Boomsma, D. I., Vink., J. M., Cornes, B. K., Martin, N. G., Skytthe, A., … de Geus, E. J. C. (2006). Genetic influence on exercise participation in 37,051 twin pairs from seven countries. *PLoS ONE*, e22, doi. org/10.1371/journal.pone.0000022.

Sue, D. W., Bingham, R. P., Porché-Burke, L., & Vasquez, M. (1999). The diversification of psychology: A multicultural revolution. *American Psychologist, 54*(12), 1061–1069.

Sullivan, M. M., & Rehm, R. (2005). Mental health of undocumented Mexican immigrants: A review of the literature. *Advances in Nursing Science, 28*, 240–251.

Sumpio, C., Jeon, S., Northouse, L. L., & Knobf, M. T. (2017). Optimism, symptom distress, illness appraisal, and coping in patients with advanced-stage cancer diagnoses undergoing chemotherapy treatment. *Oncology Nursing Forum, 44*(3), 384–392.

Sweeny, K., & Shepperd, J. A. (2010). The costs of optimism and the benefits of pessimism. *Emotion, 10*, 750–753.

Sytine, A. I., Britt, T. W., Sawhney, G., Wilson, C. A., & Keith, M. (2019). Savoring as a moderator of the daily demands and psychological capital relationship: A daily diary study. *The Journal of Positive Psychology, 14*, 641–648.

Tang, Y. Y., Hölzel, B. K., & Posner, M. I. (2015). The neuroscience of mindfulness meditation. *Nature Reviews Neuroscience, 16*, 213–225.

Tay, L., Batz, C., Parrigon, S., & Kuykendall, L. (2017). Debt and subjective well-being: The other side of the income-happiness coin. *Journal of Happiness Studies, 18*, 903–937.

Taylor, R. J., Chatters, L. M., & Levin, J. (2004) *Religion in the lives of African Americans: Social, psychological, and health perspectives.* Sage.

Taylor, S. E. (1991). Asymmetrical effects of positive and negative events: the mobilization-minimization hypothesis. *Psychological Bulletin, 110*(1), 67–85.

Taylor, S. E. (2006). Tend and befriend: Biobehavioral bases of affiliation under stress. *Current Directions in Psychological Science, 15*, 273–277.

Taylor, R. J., Chatters, L. M., Hardison, C. B., & Riley, A. (2001). Informal social support networks and subjective well-being among African Americans. *Journal of Black Psychology, 27*, 439–463.

Terman, L. M. (1922). A new approach to the study of genius. *Psychological Review, 29*, 310–318.

Terman, L. M. (1926). *Genetic studies of genius: Vol. 1. Mental and physical traits of a thousand gifted children* (2nd ed.). Stanford University Press.

Terman, L. M., & Oden, M. H. (1959). *Genetic studies of genius: Vol. 5. The gifted group at midlife.* Stanford University Press.

Teruya, S. A., & Bazargan-Hejazi, S. (2013). The immigrant and Hispanic paradoxes: A systematic review of their predictions and effects. *Hispanic Journal of Behavioral Sciences, 35*, 486–509.

Teshale, S. M., & Lachman, M. E. (2013). Managing daily happiness: The relationship between selection, optimization, and compensation strategies and well-being in adulthood. *Psychology and Aging, 31*, 687–692.

Thayer, J. F., Åhs, F., Fredrikson, M., Sollers, J. J., III, & Wager, T. D. (2012). A meta-analysis of heart rate variability and neuroimaging studies: implications for heart rate variability as a marker of stress and health. *Neuroscience & Biobehavioral Reviews, 36*, 747–756.

Thibaut, J. W., & Kelley, H. H. (1959). *The social psychology of groups.* Wiley.

Thomas, J. L., Britt, T. W., Odle-Dusseau, H., & Bliese, P. D. (2011). Dispositional optimism buffers combat veterans from the negative effects of warzone stress on mental health symptoms and work impairment. *Journal of Clinical Psychology, 67*(9), 866–880.

Thompson, K. (2016). *What percentage of your life will you spend at work?* https://revisesociology.com/2016/08/16/percentage-life-work/

Thompson, L. Y., Snyder, C. R., Hoffman, L., Michael, S. T., Rasmussen, H. N., Billings,

L. S., … Roberts, D. J. (2005). Dispositional forgiveness of self, others, and situations. *Journal of Personality, 73*, 313–359.

Thoresen, C. E. (2007). Spirituality, religion, and health: What's the deal? In T. G. Plante & C. E. Thoresen (Eds.), *Spirit, science, and health: How the spiritual mind fuels physical wellness* (pp. 3–10). Praeger.

Thornton, L. M., Cheavens, J. S., Heitzmann, C. A., Dorfman, C. S., Wu, S. M., & Andersen, B. L. (2014). Test of mindfulness and hope components in a psychological intervention for women with cancer recurrence. *Journal of Consulting and Clinical Psychology, 82*(6), 1087–1100.

Tingey, J. L., McGuire, A. P., Stebbins, O. L., & Erickson, T. M. (2019). Moral elevation and compassionate goals predict posttraumatic growth in the context of a college shooting. *Journal of Positive Psychology, 14*, 261–270.

Titova, L., Wagstaff, A. E., & Parks, A. C. (2017). Disentangling the effects of gratitude and optimism: A cross-cultural investigation. *Journal of Cross-Cultural Psychology, 48*, 754–770.

Toma, C. L., & Carlson, C. L. (2015). How do Facebook users believe they come across in their profiles? A meta-perception approach to investigating Facebook self-presentation. *Communication Research Reports, 32*(1), 93–101.

Toma, C. L., & D'Angelo, J. D. (2017). How people self-present and form impressions of others through online dating profiles. In N. M. Punyanunt-Carter & J. S. Wrench (Eds.), *The impact of social media in modern romantic relationships* (pp. 147–162). Lexington Books.

Tomasik, M. J., Napolitano, C. M., & Moser, U. (2019). Trajectories of academic performance across compulsory schooling and thriving in young adulthood. *Child Development, 90*, e745–e762.

Tomba, E., Belaise, C., Ottolini, F., Ruini, C., Bravi, A., Albieri, E., … Fava, G. A. (2010). Differential effects of well-being promoting and anxiety-management strategies in a non-clinical school setting. *Journal of Anxiety Disorders, 24*, 326–333.

Tomlinson, E. R., Yousaf, O., Vittersø, A. D., & Jones, L. (2018). Dispositional mindfulness and psychological health: A systematic review. *Mindfulness, 9*, 23–43.

Tooby, J., & Cosmides, L. (2008). The evolutionary psychology of the emotions and their relationship to internal regulatory variables. In M. Lewis, J. M. Haviland-Jones, & L. F. Barrett (Eds.), *Handbook of emotions* (pp. 114–137). Guilford Press.

Treloar, C., & Hopwood, M. (2008). "Look, I'm fit, I'm positive and I'll be all right, thank you very much": Coping with hepatitis C treatment and unrealistic optimism. *Psychology, Health & Medicine, 13*, 360–366.

Triandis, H. (1988). Collectivism v. individualism: A reconceptualisation of a basic concept in cross-cultural social psychology. In G. K. Verma & C. Bagley (Eds.), *Cross-cultural studies of personality, attitudes and cognition* (pp. 60–95). Palgrave Macmillan.

Triandis, H. C. (1995). *Individualism and collectivism*. Westview Press.

Trickett, E. J., Beehler, S., Deutsch, C., Green, L. W., Hawe, P., McLeroy, K., … Trimble, J. E. (2011). Advancing the science of community-level interventions. *American Journal of Public Health, 101*(8), 1410–1419.

Trivette, C., & Dunst, C. (2005). Community-based parent support programs. In *Encyclopedia on Early Childhood Development*. Centre of Excellence for Early Childhood Development. http://citeseerx.ist.psu.edu/viewdoc/download?doi = 10.1.1.616.1988&rep = rep1&type = pdf

Tsai, J. L., Koopmann-Holm, B., Miyazaki, M., & Ochs, C. (2013). The religious shaping of feeling. In R. F. Paloutzian & C. L Park (Eds.), *Handbook of the psychology of religion and spirituality* (pp. 274–291). Guilford Press.

Tuck, N. L., Adams, K. S., Pressman, S. D., & Cosedine, N. S. (2017). Greater ability to express positive emotion is associated with lower projected cardiovascular disease risk. *Journal of Behavioral Medicine, 40*, 855–863.

Tucker-Drob, E. M., & Bates, T. C. (2016). Large cross-national differences in gene x socioeconomic status interaction on intelligence. *Psychological Science, 27*, 138–149.

Turban, D. B., Lee, F. K., da Motta Veiga, S. P., Haggard, D. L., & Wu, S. Y. (2013). Be happy,

don't wait: The role of trait affect in job search. *Personnel Psychology, 66*, 483–514.

Tversky, A., & Kahneman, D. (1991). Loss aversion in riskless choice: A reference dependent model. *The Quarterly Journal of Economics, 106*, 1039–1061.

Umberson, D., & Montez, J. K. (2010). Social relationships and health: A flashpoint for health policy. *Journal of Health and Social Behavior, 51*(1 suppl.), S54–S66.

Uncapher, M. R., & Wagner, A. D. (2018). Minds and brains of media multitaskers: Current findings and future directions. *Proceedings of the National Academy of Sciences, 115*, 9889–9896.

United Nations. (2015). *World population ageing report*. United Nations.

United Nations. (2018). *Undata: A world of information.* http://data.un.org/Data .aspx?d = POP&f = tableCode%3A28

US Department of Transportation. (2009). *Driver distraction in commercial vehicle operations.* https://rosap.ntl.bts.gov/view/dot/17715

US Holocaust Memorial Museum. (2018). Auschwitz. In *The Holocaust encyclopedia.* www.ushmm.org/wlc/en/article .php?ModuleId = 10005189

Valliant, G. E., & Mukamal, K. (2001). Successful aging. *American Journal of Psychiatry, 158*, 839–847.

Vanassche, S., Swicegood, G., & Matthjis, K. (2013). Marriage and children as a key to happiness? Cross-national differences in the effects of marital status and children on well-being. *Journal of Happiness Studies, 14*, 501–524.

Van Boven, L., & Gilovich, T. (2003). To do or to have? That is the question. *Journal of Personality and Social Psychology, 85*, 1193–1202.

Van Cappellen, P., Rice, E. L., Catalino, L. I., & Fredrickson, B. L. (2017). Positive affective processes underlie positive health change behavior. *Psychology & Health, 33*, 77–97.

Van IJzendoorn, M. H., & Bakermans-Kranenburg, M. J. (2012). A sniff of trust: Meta-analysis of the effects of intranasal oxytocin administration on face recognition, trust to in-group, and trust to out-group. *Psychoneuroendocrinology, 37*, 438–443.

Verduyn, P., Delaveau, P., Rotgé, J.-Y., Fossati, P., & Mechelen, I. V. (2015). Determinants of emotion duration and underlying psychological and neural mechanisms. *Emotion Review, 7*, 330–335.

Verduyn, P., Ybarra, O., Résibois, M., Jonides, J., & Kross, E. (2017). Do social network sites enhance or undermine subjective well-being? A critical review. *Social Issues and Policy Review, 11*, 274–302.

Vieten, C., Scammell, S., Pierce, A., Pilato, R., Ammondson, I., Pargament, K. I., & Lukoff, D. (2016). Competencies for psychologists in the domains of religion and spirituality. *Spirituality in Clinical Practice, 3*(2), 92–114.

Vincent, J., & Glamser, F. D. (2006). Gender differences in the relative age effect among US Olympic Development Program youth soccer players. *Journal of Sports Sciences, 24*, 405–413.

Virani, S. S., Alonso, A., Benjamin, E. J., Bittencourt, M. S., Callaway, C. W., Carson, A. P., et al. (2020). Heart disease and stroke statistics – 2020 update: A report from the American Heart Association. *Circulation, 141*, e139–e596.

Vittengl, J. R., & Holt, C. S. (2000). Getting acquainted: The relationship of self-disclosure and social attraction to positive affect. *Journal of Social and Personal Relationships, 17*, 53–66.

Vogel, D., & Willems, J. (2020). The effects of making public service employees aware of their prosocial and societal impact: A microintervention. *Journal of Public Administration Research and Theory, 30*, 485–503.

Volpe, V. V., Rahal, D., Holmes, M., & Rivera, S. Z. (2018). Is hard work and high effort always healthy for Black college students? John Henryism in the face of racial discrimination. *Emerging Adulthood, 8*(3), 245–252.

Von Dawans, B., Fishbacher, U., Kirschbaum, C., Fehr, E., & Heinrichs, M. (2012). The social dimension of stress reactivity: Acute stress increases prosocial behavior in humans. *Psychological Science, 23*, 651–660.

Vroom, V. H. (1964). *Work and motivation.* Wiley.

Wade, N. G., Hoyt, W. T., Kidwell, J. E. M., & Worthington, E. L., Jr. (2014). Efficacy of psychotherapeutic interventions to promote

forgiveness: A meta-analysis. *Journal of Consulting and Clinical Psychology, 82,* 154–170.

Wadsworth, T. (2016). Marriage and subjective well-being: How and why context matters. *Social Indicators Research, 126,* 1025–1048.

Wai, J., Lubinski, D., & Benbow, C. P. (2005). Creativity and occupational accomplishments among intellectually precocious youth: An age 13 to age 33 longitudinal study. *Journal of Educational Psychology, 94,* 785–794.

Waldrop, D., Lightsey, O. R., Jr., Ethington, C. A., Woemmel, C. A., & Coke, A. L. (2001). Self-efficacy, optimism, health competence, and recovery from orthopedic surgery. *Journal of Counseling Psychology, 48*(2), 233.

Walker, D. I., Roberts, M. P., & Kristjánsson, K. (2015). Towards a new era of character education in theory and in practice. *Educational Review, 67*(1), 79–96.

Walker, M. (2017). *Why we sleep: Unlocking the power of sleep and dreams.* Scribner.

Wallace, B. A. (2013). *Meditations of a Buddhist skeptic: A manifesto for the mind sciences and contemplative practice.* Columbia University Press.

Walsh, L. C., Boehm, J. K., & Lyubomirsky, S. (2018). Does happiness promote career success? Revisiting the evidence. *Journal of Career Assessment, 26,* 199–219.

Warne, R. T. (2019). An evaluation (and vindication?) of Lewis Terman: What the father of gifted education can teach the 21st century. *Gifted Child Quarterly, 63,* 3–21.

Warneken, S. R., & Tomasello, M. (2006). Altruistic helping in human infants and young chimpanzees. *Science, 311,* 1301–1303.

Waterman, A. S. (1993). Two conceptions of happiness: Contrasts of personal expressiveness (eudaimonia) and hedonic enjoyment. *Journal of Personality and Social Psychology, 64,* 678–691.

Waterman, A. S., Schwartz, S. J., & Conti, R. (2008). The implications of two conceptions of happiness (hedonic enjoyment and eudaimonia) for the understanding of intrinsic motivation. *Journal of Happiness Studies, 9,* 41–79.

Watkins, P., Scheer, J., Ovnicek, M., & Kolts, R. (2007). The debt of gratitude: Dissociating gratitude and indebtedness. *Cognition and Emotion, 20,* 217–241.

Watkins, P. C., & Scheibe, D. (2017). Gratitude. In J. E. Maddux (Ed.), *Subjective well-being and life satisfaction* (pp. 210–229). Taylor and Francis.

Watkins, P. C., Uhder, J., & Pichinevskiy, S. (2015). Grateful recounting enhances subjective well-being: The importance of grateful processing. *The Journal of Positive Psychology, 10,* 91–98.

Watson, D., & Clark, L. A. (1997). Measurement and mismeasurement of mood: Recurrent and emergent issues. *Journal of Personality Assessment, 68,* 267–296.

Watson, D., Clark, L. A., & Tellegen, A. (1988). Development and validation of brief measures of positive and negative affect: The PANAS scales. *Journal of Personality and Social Psychology, 54,* 1063–1070.

Watson, D., & O'Hara, M. W. (2017). Positive mood dysfunction in psychopathology. In *Understanding the emotional disorders: A symptom-level approach based on the IDAS-II* (pp. 87–118). Oxford University Press.

Watten, R. G., Myhrer, T., & Swersen, J. L. (1995). Quality of life, intelligence, and mood. *Social Indicators Research, 36,* 287–299.

Wechsler, D. (2008). *Wechsler Adult Intelligence Scale* (4th ed.). Pearson.

Weden, M. M., Miles, J. N. V., Friedman, E., Escarce, J. J., Peterson, C., Langa, K. M., & Shih, R. A. (2017). The Hispanic paradox: Race/ethnicity and nativity, immigrants enclave residence, and cognitive impairment among older US adults. *Journal of the American Geriatrics Society, 65,* 1085–1091.

Weinstein, E. (2018). The social media see-saw: Positive and negative influences on adolescents' affective well-being. *New Media & Society, 20,* 3597–3623.

Weinstein, N. D. (1980). Unrealistic optimism about future life events. *Journal of Personality and Social Psychology, 39,* 806–820.

Weinstein, N. D. (1983). Reducing unrealistic optimism about illness susceptibility. *Health Psychology, 2*(1), 11–20.

Weinstein, N., Brown, K. W., & Ryan, R. M. (2009). A multi-method examination of the effects of mindfulness on stress attribution, coping, and emotional well-being. *Journal of Research in Personality*, 43, 374–385.

Weinstein, N. D., & Klein, W. M. (1995). Resistance of personal risk perceptions to debiasing interventions. *Health Psychology*, 14, 132–140.

Weiss, L. A., Westerhof, G. J., & Bohlmeijer, E. T. (2016). Can we increase psychological well-being? The effects of interventions on psychological well-being: A meta-analysis of randomized controlled trials. *PLoS ONE*, 11(6), e0158092.

Wertag, A., & Bratko, D. (2019). In search of the prosocial personality: Personality traits as predictors of prosociality and prosocial behavior. *Journal of Individual Differences*, 40, 55–62.

Westermann, A. G. (1993). The logoanchor technique. *International Forum for Logotherapy: Journal of Search for Meaning*, 16(1), 20–25.

Whillans, A. V., Dunn, E. W., Smeets, P., Bekkers, R., & Norton, M. I. (2017). Buying time promotes happiness. *Proceedings of the National Academy of Sciences*, 114, 8523–8527.

Whillans, A. V., Weidman, A. C., & Dunn, E. W. (2016). Valuing time over money is associated with greater happiness. *Social Psychological and Personality Science*, 7, 213–222.

Whisman, M. A. (2001). The association between depression and marital dissatisfaction. In S. R. H. Beach (Ed.), *Marital and family processes in depression: A scientific foundation for clinical practice* (pp. 3–24). American Psychological Association.

White, M. S., Addison, C. C., Jenkins, B. W. C., Bland, V., Clark, A., & LaVigne, D. A. (2017). Optimistic bias, risk factors, and development of high blood pressure and obesity among African American adolescents in Mississippi (USA). *International Journal of Environmental Research and Public Health*, 14, 209–220.

Whitley, E., Popham, F., & Benzeval, M. (2016). Comparison of the Rowe–Kahn model of successful aging with self-rated health and life satisfaction: The West Scotland Twenty-07 prospective cohort study. *The Gerontologist*, 56, 1082–1092.

Wiese, B. S. (2007). Successful pursuit of personal goals and subjective well-being. In B. R. Little, K. Salmela-Aro, & S. D. Phillips (Eds.), *Personality project pursuit: Goals, action, and human flourishing* (pp. 301–328). Lawrence Erlbaum.

Wiggins, J. S., & Trobst, K. K. (1997). When is a circumplex an "interpersonal circumplex"? The case of supportive actions. In R. Plutchik & H. R. Conte (Eds.), *Circumplex models of personality and emotions* (pp. 57–80). American Psychological Association.

Wight, R. G., LeBlanc, A. J., & Lee Badgett, M. V. (2013). Same-sex legal marriage and psychological well-being: Findings from the California Health Interview Survey. *American Journal of Public Health*, 103, 339–346.

Wilber, K. (1997). An integral theory of consciousness. *Journal of Consciousness Studies*, 4, 71–92.

Wilbur, R. C., & Parenté, R. (2008). A cognitive technology for fostering hope. *Cognitive Technology*, 13, 24–29.

Williams, K. (2003). Has the future of marriage arrived? A contemporary examination of gender, marriage, and psychological well-being. *Journal of Health and Social Behavior*, 44, 470–487.

Williams, L. A., & Bartlett, M. Y. (2015). Warm thanks: Gratitude expression facilitates social affiliation in new relationships via perceived warmth. *Emotion*, 15, 1–5.

Wilson, D. S. (2002). *Darwin's cathedral: Evolution, religion, and the nature of society*. University of Chicago Press.

Wojciszke, B. (2002). From the first sight to the last drop: A six stage model of the dynamics of love. *Polish Psychological Bulletin*, 33, 15–26.

Wolla, S. A., & Sullivan, J. (2017). Education, income, and wealth. *Page One Economics*. https://research.stlouisfed.org/publications/page1-econ/2017/01/03/education-income-and-wealth/

Wollburg, E., & Braukhaus, C. (2010). Goal setting in psychotherapy: The relevance of approach and avoidance goals for treatment outcome. *Psychotherapy Research*, 20, 488–494.

Wong, D. B. (2006). The meaning of detachment in Daoism, Buddhism, and Stoicism. *Dao: A Journal of Comparative Philosophy, 5*(2), 207–219.

Wood, A. M., Froh, J. J., & Geraghty, A. W. A. (2010). Gratitude and well-being: A review and theoretical integration. *Clinical Psychology Review, 30*, 890–905.

Wood, A. M., Joseph, S., Lloyd, J., & Atkins, S. (2009). Gratitude influences sleep through the mechanism of pre-sleep cognitions. *Journal of Psychosomatic Research, 66*, 43–48.

Wood, A. M., Maltby, J., Stewart, N., Linley, P. A., & Joseph, S. (2008). A social-cognitive model of trait and state levels of gratitude. *Emotion, 8*, 281–290.

World Health Organization. (2004). *Promoting mental health: Concepts, emerging evidence, practice* (Summary Report). WHO.

World Health Organization. (2011). *Mobile phone use: A growing problem of driver distraction.* WHO.

World Health Organization. (2016). *World health statistics: Monitoring health for the Sustainable Development Goals.* WHO.

Worthington, E. L., Jr. (2005). *Handbook of forgiveness.* Routledge.

Worthington, E. L., Jr., Berry, J. W., & Parrott, L., III. (2001). Unforgiveness, forgiveness, religion, and health. In T. G. Plante & A. C. Sherman (Eds.), *Faith and health: Psychological perspectives* (pp. 107–138). Guilford Press.

Worthington, E. L., Griffin, B. J., & Provencher, C. (2017). Forgiveness. In J. E. Maddux (Ed.), *Subjective well-being and life satisfaction* (pp. 148–167). Routledge.

Worthington, E. L., Jr., Sandage, S. J., & Berry, J. W. (2000). Group interventions to promote forgiveness: What researchers and clinicians ought to know. In M. E. McCullough, K. I. Pargament, & C. E. Thoresen (Eds.), *Forgiveness: Theory, research, and practice* (pp. 228–253). Guilford Press.

Wright, M. A., Wren, A. A., Somers, T. J., Goetz, M. C., Fras, A. M., Huh, B. K., … Keefe, F. J. (2011). Pain acceptance, hope, and optimism: relationships to pain and adjustment in patients with chronic musculoskeletal pain. *The Journal of Pain, 12*(11), 1155–1162.

Wrosch, C., Scheier, M. F., Carver, C. S., & Schulz, R. (2003). The importance of goal disengagement in adaptive self-regulation: When giving up is beneficial. *Self and Identity, 2*(1), 1–20.

Wrzesniewski, A., & Dutton, J. (2001). Crafting a job: Revisioning employees as active crafters of their work. *Academy of Management Review, 26*, 179–201.

Wrzesniewski, A., McCauley, C., Rozin, P., & Schwartz, B. (1997). Job, careers, and callings: People's relations to their work. *Journal of Research in Personality, 31*, 21–33.

Wylleman, P., & Reints, A. (2010). A lifespan perspective on the career of talented and elite athletes: Perspectives on high-intensity sports. *Scandinavian Journal of Medicine and Science in Sports, 20*, 88–94.

Xi, J., Lee, M., LeSuer, W., Barr, P., Newton, K., & Poloma, M. (2017). Altruism and existential well-being. *Applied Research in Quality of Life, 12*, 67–88.

Xiao, S. X., Hashi, E. C., Korous, K. M., & Eisenberg, N. (2019). Gender differences across multiple types of prosocial behavior in adolescence: A meta-analysis of the prosocial tendency measure-revised (PTM-R). *Journal of Adolescence, 77*, 41–58.

Xu, J., Murphy, J. L., Kochanek, K. D., & Bastian, B. A. (2016) Deaths: Final data for 2013. *National Vital Statistics Reports, 64*, 1–118.

Yakubovich, V., & Burg, R. (2019). Friendship by assignment? From formal interdependence to informal relations in organizations. *Human Relations, 72*, 1013–1038.

Yalçın, I., & Malkoç, A. (2015). The relationship between meaning in life and subjective well-being: Forgiveness and hope as mediators. *Journal of Happiness Studies, 16*(4), 915–929.

Yalom, I. D. (1980). *Existential psychotherapy.* Basic Books.

Yang, H., Yang, S., & Isen, A. M. (2013). Positive affect improves working memory: Implications for controlled cognitive processing. *Cognition and Emotion, 27*, 474–482.

Young, K. S., van der Velden, A. M., Craske, M. G., Pallesen, K. J., Fjorback, L., Roepstorff, A., & Parsons, C. E. (2018). The impact of mindfulness-based interventions on brain

activity: A systematic review of functional magnetic resonance imaging studies. *Neuroscience & Biobehavioral Reviews*, *84*, 424–433.

Yukl, G. A., & Latham, G. P. (1978). Interrelationships among employee participation, individual differences, goal difficulty, goal acceptance, goal instrumentality, and performance. *Personnel Psychology*, *31*, 305–323.

Zahn, R., Garrido, G., Moll, J., & Grafman, J. (2014). Individual differences in posterior cortical volume correlate with proneness to pride and gratitude. *Social Cognitive and Affective Neuroscience*, *9*, 1676–1683.

Zhang, J. Y. (2020). Grateful people are happier because they have fond memories of their past. *Personality and Individual Differences*, *152*, 109602.

Zhang, N., Ji, L-J., Bai, B., & Li, Y. (2018). Culturally divergent consequences of receiving thanks in close relationships. *Emotion*, *18*, 46–57.

Zhang, Y., & Han, B. (2016). Positive affect and mortality risk in older adults: A meta-analysis. *PsyCh Journal*, *5*, 125–138.

Zhang, Z., Zhang, L., Xiu, J., & Zheng, J. (2020). Learning from your leaders and helping your coworkers: The trickle-down effect of leader helping behavior. *Leadership and Organization Development Journal*, *41*, 883–894.

Zika, S., & Chamberlain, K. (1992). On the relation between meaning in life and psychological well-being. *British Journal of Psychology*, *83*, 133–145.

Zimbardo, P. G., & Boyd, J. N. (1999). Putting time in perspective: A valid, reliable individual-difference metric. *Journal of Personality and Social Psychology*, *77*, 1271–1288.

Zimmerman, M., McGlinchey, J. B., Posternak, M. A., Friedman, M., Attiullah, N., & Boerescu, D. (2006). How should remission from depression be defined? The depressed patient's perspective. *American Journal of Psychiatry*, *163*, 148–150.

Zimring, J. C. (2019). *What science is and how it really works*. Cambridge University Press.

Zinnbauer, B. J., Pargament, K. I., Cole, B., Rye, M. S., Butter, E. M., Belavich, T. G., … Kadar, J. L. (1997). Religion and spirituality: Unfuzzying the fuzzy. *Journal for the Scientific Study of Religion*, *36*, 549–564.

Zullow, H. (1991). Explanations and expectations: Understanding the "doing" side of optimism. *Psychological Inquiry*, *2*(1), 45–49.

Index

Page numbers in bold indicate Glossary items

acceptance, 121, **388**

acute illness risk

influence of positive affective experiences, 61–62

Adult Attachment Interview, 267

affect, **388**

affect valuation theory, 107

aging

meaning in life across the life-span, 92–95

aging successfully

Alameda 7 behaviors, 232, 233

Alameda County Study, 232

Blue Zones of successful aging, 244–246

changing demographics, 226–227

cultural contexts, 244–247

defining successful aging, 227–241

Emotional Maturity Hypothesis, 242

expand your perspective on aging, 248–250

foundational studies, 232

future research directions, 247–248

get inspired by some older folks, 250

Harvard Study of Adult Development, 231, 233–234

Hispanic Paradox (Latinx Paradox), 246–247

increasing life expectancy, 226–227

intergenerational relationships, 226

interview an older adult, 248–249

life of Sister Jean Dolores-Schmidt, 225–226

MacArthur Study, 230–231

models of successful aging, 227–228

negative stereotypes about aging, 227

positivity effect, 239–240

predictors of, 233–236

proactively cope using lessons from the Blue Zones, 249–250

Proactivity Model, 240–241

processes of, 236–241

selection–optimization–compensation model, 237–238

socioemotional selectivity theory, 238–240

well-being and aging, 241–242

why aging matters, 226–227

wisdom, 242–243

Ainsworth, Mary, 266

Alameda 7 behaviors, 232, **388**

Aldrin, Buzz, 149

Allport, Gordon, 108

Almond, Richard, 90

altruism, 311–325, **388**

competitive altruism, 313

defining, 311–312

egoism-motivated altruism, 313–316

empathy-motivated altruism, 313–316

kin altruism, 312

motivations for, 312–316

motives from evolutionary theory, 312

mutualism, 312

reciprocal altruism, 312

volunteer in your community in a way that fits your strengths, 331–332

See also prosocial behavior

anecdotal evidence, 21–22, **388**

Anjum, Afroze, 374

Antonovsky, Aaron, 91

approach goals, **388**

Aristippus, 11

Aristotle, 4, 215, 216, 368, **390**

virtue theory, 201

Armstrong, Neil, 149

attachment theory, 266–268, **388**

attitudinal values

meaning in life and, 89

attributional style. *See* explanatory styles

Attributional Style Questionnaire (ASQ), 181–182

attrition (of data), **388**

authentic happiness, **388**

Authentic Happiness (Seligman), 217, 219, 373, 374

authentic happiness model, 12

autonomy, **388**

role in satisfaction at work, 349–350

avoidance goals, **388**

Āyurveda, 103

balance theory of relationships, 270–271, **388**

Bardeen, John, 151

Battista, John, 90
Bauman, Jeff, 173
Baumeister, Roy F., 91–92
Becker, Ernest, 89
beginner's mind, 121, **388**
Behavior Risk Factor Surveillance System (BRFSS), 264
behavioral action tendency, 52, **388**
being in the zone. *See* flow state
Berlin Aging Study, 237
best possible self exercise, 386
Biles, Simone, 151
Biswas-Diener, Robert, 219
Blue Zones of successful aging, 244–246
    proactively cope using lessons from the Blue Zones, 249–250
Boo Radley Society, 384
Bowlby, John, 266
Bowles, Samuel, 349–350
brain function
    effects of mindfulness practice, 130–133
Broaden and Build Theory, 51–55, 285, 322, **388**
Buddha, 84, 85, 300
Buddhism, 14, 15, 106, 107, 109, 139–140, 190, 206
Buettner, Dan, 244–246
Buffet, Warren, 169
Byrne, Rhonda, 21–22

California Health Interview Survey (CHIS), 266
calling (related to work), **388**
Calm app, 128
Camus, Albert, 85
cardiovascular disease risk
    influence of positive affective experiences, 63
Carver, Michael F., 179–180
Cast Away (film, 2000), 260
Catholicism, 109
causal mechanisms
    examination of purported mechanisms, 28–29
    role of mediator variables, 28–29
causal relationships
    not the same as statistical correlation, 26–28
    using true experiments to test, 28
CD38 gene
    role in oxytocin secretion and regulation, 288–289
character
    advantages of good character, 215–217
    challenges of researching character, 202–215

components of, 202
cultural comparisons of character strengths, 217–220
future research directions, 220–221
historical perspectives, 201–202
identifying character strengths, 221–222
natural talents, 202–206
operational definitions, 202
personality disorders, 202
positive introduction exercise, 221
potential to use strengths for harm, 212
signature strengths, 210–211
strength spotting exercise, 221
strengths, 206–211
strengths of Fred Rogers, 199–200
use a character strength, 222
values, 212–215
Values in Action (VIA) virtues and strengths, 206–211
virtue theory, 201, 202
virtues, 206–211
well-being and good character, 215–217
why it matters, 200–201
Charlemagne, 206
Chödrön, Pema, 300
Chouinard, Yvon, 349
Christianity, 106, 107, 190, 206
    virtues, 201–202
Cicero, 281
circumplex model of emotions, 49–50
Clifton, Donald, 202–206
Clifton StrengthsFinder, 205
clinical psychology, 7, 8, 9
Clinton, Bill, 200
cognitive functioning
    influence of emotions on, 67–68
cognitive model of gratitude, **388**
cognitive behavioral therapy (CBT)
    augmentation with well-being therapy (WBT), 377–378
    strengths-based approach, 372
coherence
    sense of, 90–91
cohort effects, 95
collectivism, 14
collectivist cultures
    goals related to life satisfaction, 190–191
community initiatives, 384–385
companionate love, **389**

compassionate goals, 325–326, **389**
  moral elevation from, 326–328
confirmation bias, 22, **389**
confounder variables, 27, **389**
Confucianism, 206
contentment
  cultural perspectives, 14–15
control groups in studies, 323–325
coping behaviors
  positive and negative religious coping behaviors, 103–105
correlation coefficients
  interpretation of, 26–27
correlations, **389**
  not the same as causation, 26–28
COVID-19 pandemic
  feelings of isolation, 260
  online relationships, 275
  relevance of positive psychology, 38–39
creative values
  meaning in life and, 89
cross-sectional studies, 94–95
Csikszentmihalyi, Mihaly, 384
Cuddy, Amy, 32–33
culture
  meaning in life and, 89–90
culture and positive psychology
  aging successfully, 244–247
  Blue Zones of successful aging, 244–246
  character strengths, 217–220
  conceptualizations of mindfulness, 139–141
  contentment versus satisfaction, 14–15
  culture wars, 217
  Eastern and Western perspectives on well-being, 13–15
  gratitude, 301–302
  harmony versus mastery, 14
  Hispanic Paradox (Latinx Paradox), 246–247
  hope and optimism, 190–192
  inequity in identifying and supporting gifted individuals, 164–166
  love and marriage, 272–275
  perspective-taking, 301–302
  perspectives on happiness at work, 355–358
  positive psychology interventions (PPIs), 383–385
  prosocial behavior, 328–329
  racial happiness gap, 39–41
  religion and spirituality in different contexts, 109–111
  talent and giftedness, 164–166
  transcendence or self-enhancement, 14
  values across cultures, 217–220
  valuing or avoiding suffering, 15
  World Happiness Report, 73–75
Curie, Marie, 151, 173

daimons, 11
deliberate practice, **389**
  how to practice deliberately, 168
  role in expert performance, 158–162
Descartes, René, 370
developmental psychology, 8, 9
developmental theory, 95
dialectical behavior therapy (DBT), 380–381
Diener, Ed, 190–191
disease model, **389**
disparities between groups, **389**
dispositional optimism, **389**
Dollard, John, 175
Dolores-Schmidt, Sister Jean, 225–226
Doss, Desmond T., 83–84
Duchenne smile, 53, 64, 65, **389**

Earhart, Amelia, 173
Easterlin Paradox, 70–71, **389**
effect size, 354–355, **389**
effectiveness research, **389**
efficacy
  requirement for meaning in life, 92
efficacy expectancies, **389**
efficacy research, **389**
egoism-motivated altruism, 313–316, **389**
Ehrenreich, Barbara, 30
Elliott, Marta, 110–111
Ellis, Albert, 109
emotional contagion, 66
emotional maturity hypothesis, 242, **389**
emotions, **389**
  circumplex model of emotions, 49–50
empathy-motivated altruism, 313–316, **390**
empirical research, 23, **390**
Ericsson, K. Anders, 158–162
eudaimonia, 76–77, 201, **390**
eudaimonic well-being, 11–12, 14, **390**
evolutionary theory
  motives for prosocial behavior, 312
existential philosophy, 86
existential vacuum concept, 88–89

expectancies, **390**
 anticipating the future, 178–179
 comparison of expectancy constructs, 186
 efficacy expectancy, 179
 future research directions, 192
 outcome expectancy, 179
 valence of an outcome, 179
 See also hope; optimism
expectations
 unrealistic expectations, 188–190
experiential values
 meaning in life and, 89
experimental hypothesis, 25–26
experiments. *See* true experiments
explanatory styles, 181–182, **390**
 change your explanatory style, 193
external validity of study findings, 58
extrinsic goals, **390**
extrinsic religious orientation, **390**
eye movement desensitization and reprocessing
 (EMDR), 28–29

Fava, Giovanni, 377
Five-Factor Mindfulness Questionnaire (FFMQ),
 124
five-factor model of personality, 51
flow state, 138–139, **390**
 find flow, 144–145
forgiveness, 297–301, **390**
 decision to forgive, 300–301
 definition of, 297
 difficulty in expressing, 297–299
 forgiveness interventions, 299–301
 future research directions, 302–303
 injustice gap, 298–299
 negative effects of holding a grudge, 300
 practice forgiveness, 303–305
 REACH intervention, 299
 remember a time when you were forgiven, 305
 self-forgiveness, 298
 targets of, 297
 unforgiveness, 297
 what it is and is not, 297–299
 why perspective-taking matters, 280–281
Frankl, Viktor E., 86–89, 97, 113
Franklin, Benjamin, 206
Fredrickson, Barbara
 Broaden and Build Theory, 285, 322
 Love 2.0, 257–260, **392**

sharing positive moments, 276–277
Freud, Sigmund, 108
friendships
 influence on well-being, 261–262
Fromm, Erich, 5
frustration-aggression hypothesis, 175, **390**
future of positive psychology. *See* next steps in
 positive psychology

Gagarin, Yuri, 149
Gallup Organization, 202
generalizability of study findings, 58, **390**
genetic factors
 conserved transcriptional response to adversity
 (CTRA), 320–321
 genetic studies of genius, 163
 role in talent and giftedness, 156
giftedness. *See* talent and giftedness
Glenn, John, 149, 150
goal disengagement, **390**
goals
 approach goals versus avoidance goals, 177
 compassionate goals, 325–328
 cultural influences on, 190–192
 difficulty of, 176–177
 emotions associated with pursuit of, 174
 expectancy theory of motivation, 178–179
 factors affecting well-being, 176–177
 frustration-aggression hypothesis, 175
 future research directions, 192
 hopeful daydreaming, 195
 intrinsic versus extrinsic goals, 177
 pathways mapping, 193–194
 personal importance of, 176
 positive and negative relationships with affect,
 175–176
 problems with avoidance goals, 363–364
 real-life examples of seemingly-impossible goals
 achieved, 173–174
 self-image goals, 325
 specific versus abstract goals, 177
 why they matter, 174
Gollwitzer, Peter M., 183–184
good life
 role of positive feelings and experiences, 9
Google, 335
Gordon, Samantha, 173
gratitude, 281–297, **390**
 association with well-being, 282–288

gratitude (cont.)
    circumstances that facilitate or suppress
        gratitude, 288–291
    cognitive model, 282–285
    create a gratitude jar, 304–305
    cultural contexts, 301–302
    definitions of, 281–282
    future research directions, 302–303
    gratitude journey of A. J. Jacobs, 279–280
    influence on sleep outcomes, 283–285
    practice gratitude, 303–305
    psychosocial model, 285–288
    why it is so hard to express, 293–295
    why perspective-taking matters, 280–281
    witnessing effect, 287–288
    write and deliver a gratitude letter, 303–304
Gratitude (Sacks), 250
gratitude interventions, 291–293
    gratitude letter or gratitude visit, 291–292
    Three Good Things (Counting Blessings), 291
Gray, Thomas, "Ode on a Distant Prospect of Eton
    College", 34
Greenberg, Jeff, 89–90

happiness
    relationship to success at work,
        337–340
happiness gap, **390**
    racial disparity in happiness levels, 39–41
happiness pie, 36, **390**
    your piece of the pie, 43
happiness set point, 35–36, **390**
Harari, Yuval Noah, 212
harmony
    cultural perspectives, 14
Harris, Alex, 372
Harvard Study of Adult Development,
    233–234
Hatfield, Elaine, 255
Havighurst, Robert, 227–228
Hayward, R. David, 110–111
Headspace app, 128
healthier behavior
    association with religiousness/spirituality,
    103
hedonic adaptation, 71
hedonic treadmill, 35
hedonic well-being, 11–12, 13, **391**
hedonism, 11, 48, **391**

Heidegger, Martin, 85
Hendrick, Clyde, 255–256, **392**
Hendrick, Susan, 255–256, **392**
Hidden Figures (Margot Lee Shetterly), 149
Hilton, 335
Hinduism, 15, 103, 206
Hispanic Paradox, 246–247
history of positive psychology, 3–7
hope, 182–185
    comparison of expectancy constructs, 186
    cultural contexts, 190–192
    examples in popular culture, 173
    future research directions, 192
    hopeful daydreaming, 195
    trait versus state measures, 184–185
    unrealistic expectations, 188–190
    well-being and, 186–187
    why it matters, 174
Hope Scale, 184
hope theory, 375, **391**
    goals, pathways, and agency, 183–184
    work of C. R. Snyder, 183–184
hope therapy, 375–377
    agency techniques, 377
    example (Amy), 363–364
    goal techniques, 376
    pathways techniques, 376–377
hopeful daydreaming exercise, 386–387
Hoyt, Rick and Dick, 326
humanistic psychology, 5–6
hypothesis testing, 24–26
    experimental hypothesis, 25–26
    null hypothesis, 25–26

idiographic research, 271–272, **391**
individualism, 14
individualist cultures
    goals related to life satisfaction, 190–191
industrial/organizational psychology, 8, 9
inflammatory response
    influence of positive affective experiences, 62–63
Inside Out (movie), 47–48
intelligence (IQ)
    genetic studies of genius, 163
interdisciplinary nature of positive psychology, 7–9
intergenerational relationships, **391**
internal validity of study findings, 57–58
interpersonal relationships
    trait mindfulness research, 125–126

interrater reliability, 31

intersectionality, **391**

   influences on happiness, 40

intrinsic goals, **391**

intrinsic religious orientation, **391**

investment theory of commitment, 269, **391**

Isen, Alice M., 67–68

Islam, 107, 206

Jackson, Mary, 149

Jacobs, A. J.

   gratitude journey of, 279–280

James, William, 4, 99

Jesus, 85

job crafting, 351–353, 359–360, **391**

John Henryism, 191–192, **391**

Johnson, Katherine, 149–150

Journal of Happiness Studies, 16

Journal of Positive Psychology, 16

Judaism, 106, 107, 190, 206

Kabat-Zinn, Jon, 118, **392**

Keyes, Corey, 366

Kierkegaard, Søren, 85

kindness, 311–325

   competitive altruism, 313

   defining kindness, 311–312

   kin altruism, 312

   kindness interventions, 321–323

   motivations for, 312–316

   motives from evolutionary theory, 312

   mutualism, 312

   put kindness into the world, 330–331

   reciprocal altruism, 312

   See also prosocial behavior

King, Martin Luther, Jr., 117

Koenig, Harold G., 101–102

Krasinski, John, 326

Langer, Ellen, 121–123

Lao Tzu, 85

Latinx Paradox, 246–247

law of attraction, 21–22

learned helplessness, 180–181, **391**

learned optimism, 180–182, **391**

Lee, John Alan, 255

LGB couples

   impact of marital status on psychological well-being, 265–266

Life Attitudes Profile (LAP), 93

LIFE model, 370–373, **391**

Life Orientation Test (LOT), 32, 179–180, 182

Life Orientation Test–Revised (LOT-R), 31–32

Little, Brian R., 176

Locus of Hope Scale, 192

logoanchor technique, 113

logotherapy, 86–89, **391**

Lomas, Tim, 370

longevity

   association with religiousness/spirituality, 102–103

longitudinal studies, 94–95, **391**

Lopez, Shane, 372

Love 2.0, **392**

love and relationships

   attachment theory, 266–268

   balance theory of relationships, 270–271

   companionate love, 255

   cultural contexts, 272–275

   friendships, 261–262

   future research directions, 275

   impact of one's social network on happiness, 260–261

   importance of friendships, 253–254

   influence of vagal tone, 259–260

   investment theory of commitment, 269

   Love 2.0, 257–260

   love songs, 254

   love styles, 255–256

   make a connection, 276–277

   marital status and psychological well-being, 263–266

   meanings of love, 254–260

   online relationships, 262–263

   passionate love, 255

   positivity resonance (synchronous brain activity), 258–259

   practice positive relationships, 275–277

   rebalance your relationships, 275–276

   role of oxytocin, 259, 276

   social exchange theories, 268–270

   Tag Brothers, 253–254

   theoretical models of what makes for good relationships, 266–272

   triangular theory of love, 256–257

   types of love, 254–260

   well-being and relationships, 260–266

   why they matter, 254

Love Attitude Scale (LAS), 256
love styles, **392**
loving kindness meditations (LKM), 127, **392**
Lyubomirsky, Sonja, 373

Making Hope Happen (Lopez, 2013), 373
Mandela, Nelson, 173, 300
marital status
    influence on psychological well-being, 263–266
Marlowe–Crowne Social Desirability Index
        (MCSDI), 209–210
Maslow, Abraham, 5
Maslow's hierarchy of needs
    relationship to positive psychological states,
        38–39
    transcendence, 84–85
mastery
    cultural perspectives, 14
maturation effects, 94–95
meaning in life, 11–13, 85–98, **392**
    across the life-span, 92–95
    culture and, 89–90
    defining meaning, 86
    defining purpose, 86
    defining significance, 86
    four needs for meaning, 91–92
    Logotherapy, 86–89
    need for efficacy, 92
    need for purpose, 91–92
    need for self-worth, 92
    need for value, 92
    paradoxical search for, 97–98
    psychological processes that lead to, 86
    relationship to well-being, 95–97
    self-esteem and, 90
    sense of coherence (SOC), 90–91
    terror management theory (TMT), 89–90
    theories of, 86–92
    values and, 89
    See also transcendence
Meaning in Life Questionnaire (MLQ), 11, 93, 98
measurement
    assessing positive affective experiences, 76–77
    multimodal assessment, 65–67
media multitasking, 118–119, **392**
mediation effects, 132–133
mediator variables, 28–29, **392**
mental health
    components of, 365–367

defining, 365–367
disease model, 364–365
strengths-based model, 365
why a positive approach matters, 364–365
See also positive approach to mental health
mental health interventions
    hope therapy example (Amy), 363–364
    problems with avoidance goals, 363–364
    See also positive psychology interventions;
        practice positive psychology
mental rehearsal
    hopeful daydreaming, 195
meta-analysis, **392**
methodology
    cohort effects, 95
    control groups, 323–325
    correlation does not equal causation, 295–297
    cross-sectional studies, 94–95
    effect size, 354–355
    generalizability of study findings, 231–232
    hypothesis testing, 24–26
    interpretation of correlation coefficients, 26–27
    longitudinal studies, 94–95
    maturation effects, 94–95
    mediation effects, 132–133
    moderation effects, 132–133
    multimodal assessment, 65–67
    nomothetic versus idiographic research
        perspective, 271–272
    randomization, 323–325
    relative versus absolute data, 211
    reliability of measures, 154–155
    reproducibility and replicability of studies,
        381–382
    research issues in the psychology of religion,
        106–109
    state versus trait measures, 185
    statistical significance of data, 24–26
    validity of measures, 154–155
metta meditations, **392**
Miller, Neal, 175
Million Women Study (UK), 58–59
Mills College Yearbook study, 64
mindfulness
    acceptance, 121
    attention focus practice, 127
    beginner's mind, 121
    benefits of, 123–130
    cultural conceptualizations, 139–141

definitions of, 120–122

effects on brain function, 130–133

future research and developments, 141–142

influence of evaluations and categorizations, 121–123

interpersonal relationships and trait mindfulness, 125–126

life and work of Thích Nhất Hạnh, 117–118

loving-kindness meditations (LKM), 127

mindfulness interventions research, 123–124, 127–130

mindfulness practice resources, 143

mindfulness-based stress reduction (MBSR), 128

nonjudgmental stance, 120–121

nonreactivity, 121

open awareness practice (expansive attention focus), 127

openness to novelty and newness, 121–123

physical functioning and mindfulness interventions, 128–129

present-moment awareness, 120

psychological functioning and mindfulness interventions, 129–130

psychological health and trait mindfulness, 124–125

purposeful awareness, 120

trait mindfulness research, 123–126

See also present-moment focus

Mindfulness Attention Awareness Scale (MAAS), 123

mindfulness-based stress reduction (MBSR), 118, 128, **392**

moderation effects, 132–133

moderator variables, **392**

money and happiness, 68–73

buying time, 72

income and happiness, 69–71

spend your money happily, 79

spending money as a source of happiness, 71–73

spending money on others, 72–73

mood states, 50–51

moods, **392**

moral elevation, 326–328, **392**

mortality

influence of positive affective experiences, 55–59

Moses, 85

Mr Roger's Neighborhood, 199–200

Muhammad, 85

multimodal assessment, 65–67, **392**

multimodal research design, **392**

multitasking, 118–119

myths about positive psychology

check your beliefs, 42–43

examine how you came to believe a myth, 42

how they come about, 33

only the stupid are happy, 33–34

positive psychology is only about being happy, 37–38

positive psychology is only for the privileged, 38–39

you can't do anything about your happiness, 35–36

negative emotions

role in positive psychology, 37–38

negative emotions and events

human bias toward noticing, 9

neuroscience, 8, 9

next steps in positive psychology, 15–16

assessing positive affective experiences, 76–77

character strengths, virtues, and values, 220–221

forgiveness, 302–303

goals and expectancies, 192

gratitude, 302–303

happiness at work, 358–359

love and relationships, 275

mindfulness research, 141–142

perspective-taking, 302–303

positive affective experiences, 76–78

positive psychology interventions (PPIs), 385–386

prosocial behavior, 329–330

religious and spiritual issues, 111–112

science of positive psychology, 41–42

successful aging, 247–248

talent and giftedness, 166–168

transcendence research and applications, 111–112

upregulating positive emotions, 77–78

Nietzsche, Friedrich, 85, 88

nomothetic research, 271–272, **392**

nonjudgmental stance, 120–121, **392**

nonreactivity, 121, **392**

noögenic neurosis, 88–89, **393**

null hypothesis, 25–26

Nun Study, 55–58

Obama, Barack, 150, 182

Oettingen, Gabriele, 231–232

Oishi, Shigehiro, 190–191

operational definition, **393**

optimism, 179–182
   change your explanatory style, 193
   comparison of expectancy constructs, 186
   cultural contexts, 190–192
   definition of, 179
   dispositional optimism, 179–180
   examples in popular culture, 173
   explanatory styles, 181–182
   future research directions, 192
   John Henryism, 191–192
   learned helplessness, 180–181
   learned optimism, 180–182
   Life Orientation Test–Revised (LOT-R), 179–180, 182
   real-life examples of seemingly impossible goals achieved, 173–174
   relationship to pessimism, 180
   unrealistic expectations, 188–190
   well-being and, 186–187
   why it matters, 174
optimism bias, 188–190, **396**
organizational citizenship behaviors (OCBs), 345–347, **393**
other interest, **394**
outcome expectancies, **393**
Overmier, J. Bruce, 181
oxytocin, 259, 276
   function of the CD38 gene, 288–289

p-value, 25
Panic! at the Disco, 173
Pargament, Kenneth, 100–101, 103–105, 108–109
Park, Nansook, 217
passionate love, **393**
Patagonia (company), 349
pathways mapping, 193–194
Pauling, Linus, 151
Pearson correlation coefficient (r), 27, **393**
performance expectancies, **389**
PERMA model, 12–13, **393**
   applying to your own life, 16–17
personal wisdom, **393**
personality disorders, 202
personality psychology, 8, 9
personality traits, 51
   associated with prosocial behavior, 319
perspective-taking, **393**
   cultural contexts, 301–302
   forgiveness, 297–301

future research directions, 302–303
gratitude, 281–297
   gratitude journey of A. J. Jacobs, 279–280
   practice gratitude and forgiveness, 303–305
   why it matters, 280–281
pessimism, 180
Peter Principle, **393**
   promotion at work, 350–351
Peterson, Christopher, 202, 206–211, 217, 367–368
phenomenology, **393**
physical functioning and mindfulness interventions, 128–129
physical health
   influence of positive affective experiences, 59–63
pillars of positive psychology, 7
Pillemer, Karl, 248–249
Plato, 11, **390**
pleasurable sensations, 49
pleasurable sensations toolbox
   inducing positive emotions, 79
Portrait of Values Questionnaire (PVQ), 214–215
positive activity interventions (PAIs), 373–375, **393**
positive affective experiences
   acute illness risk and, 61–62
   benefits of, 55–73
   broaden and build theory, 51–55
   cardiovascular disease risk and, 63
   circumplex model of emotions, 49–50
   defining, 49–51
   emotional contagion, 66
   functions of, 51–55
   income and happiness, 69–71
   inflammatory response and, 62–63
   influence on cognitive functioning, 67–68
   influence on mortality, 55–59
   influence on physical health, 59–63
   influence on social relationships, 64–67
   information from smiles, 64–66
   life evaluation across cultures, 73–75
   measurement of, 65–67, 76–77
   money and happiness, 68–73
   mood states, 50–51
   multimodal assessment, 65–67
   personality traits, 51
   pleasurable sensations, 49
   positive emotions, 49–50
   spending money as a source of happiness, 71–73
   temporal dimensions, 49–51
   undoing hypothesis, 61

upregulating positive emotions, 77–78

upward spiral theory of lifestyle change, 60–61

why positive emotions matter, 48

World Happiness Report, 73–75

positive affective experiences diary, 78

positive affectivity (personality trait), **393**

Positive and Negative Affect Schedule (PANAS), 11, 59

positive approach to mental health

approach to assessment and diagnosis, 364–365

components of mental health, 365–367

disease model of mental health, 364–365

hope therapy example (Amy), 363–364

problems with avoidance goals, 363–364

strengths-based assessment, 367–368

strengths-based model of mental health, 365

why it matters, 364–365

positive emotional experiences

role in the emotional landscape, 47–48

positive individual traits, 7

positive introduction exercise, 221

positive legacy exercise, 17

positive-negative asymmetry affect, **393**

positive psychological states

association with religion/spirituality, 106

positive psychology, **393**

counterbalance to negative bias in psychology, 9

history of, 3–7

interdisciplinary nature of, 7–9

origin of the term, 5

scope of, 7–9

three pillars of, 7

value of positive feelings and experiences, 9

why we need it, 9

positive psychology interventions (PPIs), 369–373, **393**

approach to assessment and diagnosis, 367–368

best possible self exercise, 386

community initiatives, 384–385

cultural contexts, 383–385

defining criteria of, 369–370

future research directions, 385–386

hope therapy, 375–377

hopeful daydreaming exercise, 386–387

identify and nurture your strengths, 374

interventions to decrease negative affect and experience, 377–382

interventions to increase positive affect and experiences, 373–375

LIFE model, 370–373

positive activity interventions (PAIs), 373–375

positive psychotherapy (PPT), 379–381

problems with over- or underuse of strengths, 367–368

strengths-based assessment, 367–368

techniques, 386–387

well-being therapy (WBT), 377–378

why they work, 382–383

positive psychotherapy (PPT), 379–381

positive social institutions, 7

positive subjective experiences, 7

positivity effect, **393**

in older adults, 239–240

positivity ratio, 79–80

power distance, **393**

power-posing craze, 32–33

practice positive psychology

apply the PERMA model to your own life, 16–17

applying scientific reasoning, 42–43

appreciate the achievements of others, 169

bring your values to work, 360–361

catch people being their best selves, 332

change your explanatory style, 193

character strength spotting, 221

check your beliefs, 42–43

create a gratitude jar, 304–305

create a movie of your life, 113–114

discover your best possible self, 386

engage in hopeful daydreaming, 386–387

engaging in positive affective experiences, 78–80

evaluate your positivity ratio, 79–80

examine how you came to believe a myth, 42

expand your perspective on aging, 248–250

explore your positive legacy, 17

find flow, 144–145

find mentors, 169–170

forgiveness, 303–305

get inspired by some older folks, 250

gratitude, 303–305

happiness at work, 359–361

hopeful daydreaming, 195

identifying character strengths, 221–222

integrate positive psychology into your life, 17

interview an older adult, 248–249

job crafting, 359–360

logoanchor technique, 113

make a connection, 276–277

make a friend at work, 360

practice positive psychology (cont.)
  meditate on the present moment, 143
  mindfulness practice resources, 143
  optimism and hope, 193–195
  pathways mapping, 193–194
  pleasurable sensations toolbox to induce
    positive emotions, 79
  positive affective experiences diary, 78
  positive introduction, 221
  positive psychology intervention (PPI)
    techniques, 386–387
  positive relationships, 275–277
  practice deliberately, 168
  present-moment focus, 143–145
  proactively cope using lessons from the Blue
    Zones, 249–250
  prosocial behavior, 330–332
  put kindness into the world, 330–331
  rebalance your relationships, 275–276
  remember a time when you were forgiven, 305
  savor the past, present, and future, 144
  spend your money happily, 79
  talent and achievement, 168–170
  transcendence, 113–114
  use a character strength, 222
  use social media in a positive way, 276
  volunteer in your community in a way that fits
    your strengths, 331–332
  write and deliver a gratitude letter, 303–304
  your piece of the happiness pie, 43
predictive use of data, **393**
present-moment awareness, 120, **393**
present-moment focus
  effects of multitasking, 118–119
  flow state, 138–139
  life and work of Thích Nhất Hạnh, 117–118
  practice of, 143–145
  savoring, 133–138
  why it matters, 118–119
  See also mindfulness
proactivity model of successful aging, 240–241, **394**
prosocial behavior, **394**
  altruism, 311–325
  circumstances most likely to produce, 319–320
  compassionate goals, 325–326
  conserved transcriptional response to adversity
    (CTRA), 320–321
  cultural contexts, 328–329
  defining altruism, 311–312

  defining kindness, 311–312
  egoism-motivated altruism, 313–316
  empathy-motivated altruism, 313–316
  fundraising work of Tyler Stallings, 309–310
  future research directions, 329–330
  in the workplace, 343–348
  kindness, 311–325
  kindness interventions, 321–323
  mechanisms of effects on well-being, 320–321
  moral elevation, 326–328
  motivations for, 312–316
  motives from evolutionary theory, 312
  people most likely to engage in, 318–319
  personality traits associated with, 319
  practice prosocial behavior, 330–332
  psychological motives for, 313–316
  singularity effect of identifiable victims, 328–329
  well-being and, 316–318
  why it matters, 310–311
prosocial impact (in work), **395**
prosocial motives, **394**
psychological functioning
  mindfulness interventions research, 129–130
psychological health
  trait mindfulness research, 124–125
psychological tests
  validity and reliability of, 31–32
psychosocial model of gratitude, **394**
psychotherapy
  positive psychotherapy (PPT), 379–381
purpose in life, **394**
  defining, 86
  requirement for meaning in life, 91–92
Purpose in Life Questionnaire, 11
purposeful awareness, 120
Pyszczynski, Tom, 89–90

quest religious orientation, **394**

racial disparity
  happiness gap, 39–41
Randi, James, 22
randomization in studies, 323–325
Rashid, Tayyab, 374, 379–380
rational emotive behavior therapy, 109
RCOPE (measure of religious coping), 101
relationships. *See* love and relationships
relative age effect, 157, **394**
relative centrality of work (RCW), **394**

reliability of measures, 31, 154–155, **394**

religion, **394**

religious and spiritual transcendence

  association with healthier behavior, 103

  common characteristics across denominations, 107–108

  distinction between religion and spirituality, 99–101

  example of Private First Class Desmond T. Doss, 83–84

  intrinsic, extrinsic and quest religious orientations, 108

  positive and negative religious coping behaviors, 103–105

  positive psychological states, 106

  purpose of psychological research on religion, 108–109

  relationship between religiousness/spirituality and longer life, 102–103

  religion is neither all good nor all bad, 107

  research issues in the psychology of religion, 106–109

  social support associated with religion/ spirituality, 105–106

  value of religion and spirituality in people's lives, 98–99

  well-being and religion/spirituality, 101–106

religious coping, **394**

replicability of study results, 32–33, **394**

  crisis in psychology, 381–382

reproducibility of studies, 381–382

Rogers, Carl, 5

Rogers, Fred, 199–200

Rogue One: A Star Wars Story, 173

Rokeach, Milton

  taxonomy of values, 212–213

Ross, J. Michael, 108

Rusbult, Caryl, 269–270, **391**

Ryff, Carol, 377

same-sex couples

  impact of marital status on psychological well-being, 265–266

Sanger, Frederick, 151

Sartre, Jean-Paul, 85

satisfaction

  cultural perspectives, 14–15

Satisfaction with Life Scale (SWLS), 11, 215

savoring, 133–138, **394**

  anticipation, 134

reminiscing, 134

savor the past, present, and future, 144

Scale of Positive and Negative Experiences, 49

Scheier, Charles S., 179–180

Schwartz, Shalom H.

  theory of basic human values, 213–215

Schwartz Value Survey (SVS), 214

science of positive psychology

  applying scientific reasoning, 42–43

  avoiding confirmation bias, 22

  conclusions based on scientific method, 23–26

  confounder variables, 27

  correlation does not equal causation, 26–28

  criticism of the law of attraction, 21–22

  cultural research, 39–41

  distinguishing from nonscientific pop psychology, 23–33

  empirical research, 23

  examination of purported causal mechanisms, 28–29

  eye movement desensitization and reprocessing (EMDR), 28–29

  generalization of results, 29–30

  hypothesis testing, 24–26

  issues with anecdotal evidence, 21–22

  next steps, 41–42

  p-value, 25

  racial happiness gap, 39–41

  replicability of study results, 32–33

  role of mediator variables, 28–29

  statistical significance of data, 24–26

  testing for causal relationships, 28

  true experiments, 28

  valid and reliable measures, 30–32

  why a scientific approach matters, 21–22

  See also myths about positive psychology

science of well-being, 11–13

scientific method, 23–26, **394**

scope of positive psychology, 7–9

selection bias, **394**

selection–optimization–compensation (SOC) model, 237–238, **394**

Selection Research Inc., 202

self

  notion of, 14

self-determination theory, 349

self-enhancement

  cultural perspectives, 14

self-esteem
    meaning in life and, 90
    sense of control and, 90–91
self-image goals, 325, **394**
self-transcendence. *See* transcendence
self-worth
    requirement for meaning in life, 92
Seligman, Martin E. P., 3–4, 7, 202, 217, 367, 384
    authentic happiness model, 12
    learned optimism, 180–182
    PERMA model, 12–13
    strengths and virtues, 206–211
sensations of pleasure, **395**
sense of coherence (SOC), 90–91, **395**
Shepard, Alan, 150
Short Schwartz Value Survey (SSVS), 214
significance in life, **395**
significance of a life
    defining, 86
Sinatra, Frank, 173
singularity effect of identifiable victims, 328–329,
    395
Sisyphus, 85
Sloan, David, 212
smiles
    information from analysis of, 64–66
Snyder, C. R., 90–91, 183–184, 192
social desirability bias, 210, **395**
social exchange theories of relationships, 268–270
social exchange theory, **395**
social media
    online relationships, 262–263
    using in a positive way, 276
social network
    impact on happiness, 260–261
social psychology, 8, 9
social relationships
    influence of positive affective experiences, 64–67
social support
    association with religion/spirituality, 105–106
societal impact (in work), **395**
socioemotional selectivity theory, 238–240, **395**
Solomon, Sheldon, 89–90
Sorokowski, Piotr, 257
spirituality, **395**
    See also religious and spiritual transcendence
Stallings, Tyler, 309–310
State Hope Scale, 184
state versus trait measures, 185

statistical significance, 24–26, **395**
    p-value, 25
Sternberg, Robert, 256–257
Sternberg's Triangular Love Scale (STLS), 257
strength of character, **395**
strengths-based assessment, 367–368
strengths-based model, **395**
strengths-based therapies, **395**
StrengthsFinder 2.0., 205
stress
    positive effects of religion/spirituality, 106
Study of Mathematically Precocious Youth
    (SMPY), 163–165
subjective well-being, 11, 13, **395**
suffering
    cultural perspectives on, 15
supernormal human functioning, 7

Tag Brothers, 253–254
talent, **395**
talent and giftedness
    appreciate the achievements of others, 169
    behavioral factors, 158–162
    biological factors, 156–157
    cultural contexts, 164–166
    defining, 152–155
    educational initiatives for high-achieving
        students, 162
    extraordinary talent of Katherine Johnson,
        149–150
    find mentors, 169–170
    future research directions, 166–168
    genetic factors in, 156
    genetic studies of genius, 163
    heritability of, 156
    how to practice deliberately, 168
    identifying and developing, 155–162
    link between educational success and life
        outcomes, 152
    longitudinal studies associated with early talent
        and giftedness, 162–164
    natural talents, 202–206
    nurturing and promotion of, 149–150
    people behind the Space Race, 149–150
    practices directed toward achievement, 168–170
    racial and ethnic bias in identification and
        support programs, 164–166
    recognition of, 149–150
    relative age effect, 157

role of deliberate practice in expert performance, 158–162

standardized testing, 152–153

Study of Mathematically Precocious Youth (SMPY), 163–165

why they matter, 151–152

Taoism, 15, 206

taxonomy, **395**

tend and befriend hypothesis, 319

Tereshkova, Valentina, 149

Terman, Lewis, 163

terror management theory (TMT), 89–90, **395**

test–retest reliability, 31

The Devil's Dictionary (Bierce), 33–34

The How of Happiness (Lyubomirsky, 2008), 373

The Little Engine That Could (Piper), 184

The Secret (Byrne), 21–22

theory of basic human values, 213–215

Thích Nhất Hạnh, 117–118

Thorsten, Carl, 372

threshold theory, **395**

time scarcity, 72

transcendence, **396**

  create a movie of your life, 113–114

  cultural contexts, 109–111

  cultural perspectives, 14

  defining, 84–85

  example of Private First Class Desmond T. Doss, 83–84

  future research and applications, 111–112

  logoanchor technique, 113

  Maslow's hierarchy of needs, 84–85

  practice of, 113–114

  why it matters, 84–85

  See also meaning in life; religious and spiritual transcendence

triangular theory of love, **396**

true experiments, 28, **396**

Tuesdays with Morrie (Albom), 250

Tyson, Neil deGrasse, 151

undoing hypothesis, **396**

unrealistic optimism, **396**

upward spiral theory of lifestyle change, 60–61, **396**

vagal tone

  influence on emotion regulation, 259–260

valence, **396**

validity of measures, 31–32, 154–155, **396**

value

  requirement for meaning in life, 92

values, 212–215, **396**

  bring your values to work, 360–361

  cross-cultural comparisons, 217–220

  definition of a value, 212

  future research directions, 220–221

  instrumental values, 213

  meaning in life and, 89

  purpose of, 212

  Rokeach taxonomy, 212–213

  Schwartz taxonomy, 213–215

  taxonomies of basic values, 212–215

  tensions between different value systems, 212

  terminal values, 212

Values in Action (VIA) system

  Inventory of Strengths (VIA-IS), 209–211

  problems with over- or underuse of strengths, 367–368

  virtues and strengths, 206–211

Vaughan, Dorothy, 149

virtue theory, 201, 202

virtues, 206–211, **396**

  cardinal virtues, 201

  future research directions, 220–221

  historical perspectives, 201–202

  theological virtues, 201

Vroom, Victor H., 178–179

Walster, G. William, 255

Wegman's Food Market, 335–336

Weinstein, Neil D., 188, 189

well-being

  aging and, 241–242

  association with good character, 215–217

  emotional maturity hypothesis, 242

  eudaimonic well-being, 11–12, 14

  hedonic well-being, 11–12, 13

  hope and, 186–187

  impact of one's social network, 260–261

  influence of friendships, 261–262

  influence of gratitude on, 282–288

  link with religion/spirituality, 101–106

  online relationships and, 262–263

  optimism and, 186–187

  prosocial behavior and, 316–318

  relationship to meaning in life, 95–97

  relationships and, 260–266

  role of positive feelings and experiences, 9

well-being (cont.)
  science of, 11–13
  subjective well-being, 11, 13
well-being therapy (WBT), 377–378
Wells, H. G., 173
Wilber, Ken, 370
wisdom
  aging and, 242–243
witnessing effect (of gratitude), **396**
Won't You Be My Neighbor?, 199–200
work
  amount of time spent working in a lifetime, 336
  bring your values to work, 360–361
  cultural perspectives on happiness at work,
    355–358
  demonstrating trust in employees, 349–350
  employees' need for autonomy, 349–350
  experienced as a job, a career, or a calling,
    341–343
  future research on happiness at work,
    358–359
  intrinsic motivation for, 349–350
  job crafting, 351–353, 359–360
  make a friend at work, 360
  make social connections, 353–354
  organizational citizenship behaviors (OCBs),
    345–347
  percentage of employees not engaged with their
    work, 336–337
  practice positive psychology at work, 359–361

promotion and the Peter Principle, 350–351
  prosocial behaviors, 345–347
  prosocial impact of, 347–348
  prosocial motives, 344–345
  prosociality in the workplace, 343–348
  provide opportunities that match strengths,
    350–351
  relationship between happiness and success at
    work, 337–340
  relative centrality of work, 356–358
  societal impact of, 347–348
  surveys of happiness at work, 335
  treating people well at Wegman's Food Market,
    335–336
  what employees can do to create a positive work
    experience, 351–355
  what employers can do to create a positive work
    environment, 348–351
  why happiness at work matters, 336–337
  work–family conflict, 355–356
work as calling theory (WCT), 341–343
work–family conflict (WFC), **396**
World Happiness Report, 73–75
World War II
  influence on the direction of psychology, 4–5

Young@Heart Chorus, 250
Yousafzai, Malala, 173–174

Zimbardo Time Perspective Inventory, 283